Let's Explore Light

by Walt K. Moon

BUMBA BOOKS™

LERNER PUBLICATIONS ◆ MINNEAPOLIS

Note to Educators:

Throughout this book, you'll find critical thinking questions. These can be used to engage young readers in thinking critically about the topic and in using the text and photos to do so.

Lerner Publications Company
A division of Lerner Publishing Group, Inc.
241 First Avenue North
Minneapolis, MN 55401 USA

For reading levels and more information, look up this title at www.lernerbooks.com.

Library of Congress Cataloging-in-Publication Data

Names: Moon, Walt K., author.
Title: Let's explore light / by Walt K. Moon.
Description: Minneapolis : Lerner Publications, [2018] | Series: Bumba books.
  First look at physical science | Audience: Ages 4–7. | Audience:
  K to Grade 3. | Includes bibliographical references and index.
Identifiers: LCCN 2017019797 (print) | LCCN 2017024751 (ebook) | ISBN
  9781512482744 (eb pdf) | ISBN 9781512482706 (lb : alk. paper) | ISBN
  9781541510838 (pb : alk. paper)
Subjects: LCSH: Light—Juvenile literature.
Classification: LCC QC360 (ebook) | LCC QC360 .M67 2018 (print) | DDC
  535—dc23

LC record available at https://lccn.loc.gov/2017019797

Manufactured in the United States of America
1 – CG – 12/31/17

Expand learning beyond the printed book. Download free, complementary educational resources for this book from our website, www.lernerresource.com.

Table of Contents

What Is Light?

Light shines.

It lets people see things.

The sun gives off light.

It shines on Earth.

Light bulbs also give off light.

What other things in the sky give off light?

Light passes through transparent objects.

Glass and plastic are transparent.

We can see through them.

What other objects are transparent?

8

Some objects are opaque.

They block light.

Light cannot pass through them.

Can you name some objects that are opaque?

Blocking light makes

a shadow.

The light cannot reach

this area.

Light bounces off a mirror.

A mirror sends light in a new direction.

Sunlight helps plants grow.

It shines on the leaves.

Leaves use energy from

sunlight to make food.

The sun shines light on the moon.

The moon looks bright from Earth.

Light helps people see in the dark.

Light bulbs and lamps help people see at night.

When do you use light?

Picture Quiz

Which items are transparent? Which are opaque?

Picture Glossary

energy

power

opaque

not clear enough to let light through

shadow

an area of shade made by something blocking out light

transparent

clear so light can pass through

23

Read More

Claybourne, Anna. *Light and Dark*. Laguna Hills, CA: QEB Publishing, 2016.

Johnson, Robin. *What Are Light Waves?* New York: Crabtree Publishing Company, 2014.

Pfeffer, Wendy. *Light Is All Around Us*. New York: HarperCollins, 2014.

Index

Photo Credits

The images in this book are used with the permission of: © Alena Ozerova/Shutterstock.com, pp. 4–5; © Evdokimov Maxim/Shutterstock.com, p. 6; © Dragon Images/Shutterstock.com, pp. 9, 23 (bottom right); © Serhiy Kobyakov/Shutterstock.com, pp. 10, 23 (top right); © altanaka/Shutterstock.com, pp. 12–13, 23 (bottom left); © Martyn F. Chillmaid/Science Source, p. 14; © Smileus/iStock.com, pp. 16–17, 23 (top left); © Ricardo Reitmeyer/Shutterstock.com, p. 18; © Yuganov Konstantin/Shutterstock.com, p. 21; © rangizzz/Shutterstock.com, p. 22 (top left); © Lipskiy/Shutterstock.com, p. 22 (top right); © Vitaly Korovin/Shutterstock.com, p. 22 (bottom left); © ESB Professional/Shutterstock.com, p. 22 (bottom right).

Front Cover: © ktsimage/iStock.com.